A Note

RUDOLF STEINE
spiritual philosophy
be understood as 'wisdom of the human being'. A highly developed seer, Steiner based his work on direct knowledge and perception of spiritual dimensions. He initiated a modern and universal 'science of spirit', accessible to anybody willing to exercise clear and unprejudiced thinking.

From his spiritual investigations, Steiner provided suggestions for the renewal of many activities, including education—both general and special—agriculture, medicine, economics, architecture, science, philosophy, religion and the arts. Today there are literally thousands of schools, clinics, farms and other organizations doing practical work based on his principles. His many published works (writings and lectures) also feature his research into the spiritual nature of the human being, the evolution of the world and humanity, and methods of personal development. Steiner wrote some 30 books and delivered over 6,000 lectures across Europe. In 1924 he founded the General Anthroposophical Society, which today has branches throughout the world.

Also in the *Meditations* series:

Meditations for Courage and Tranquility, The Heart of Peace
Meditations for Harmony and Healing, Finding the Greater Self
Meditations for the Dead, Connecting to those who have Died

MEDITATIONS
for Times of Day and Seasons of the Year

Breathing the Spirit

Rudolf Steiner

Edited and translated
by Matthew Barton

Sophia Books

An imprint of Rudolf Steiner Press

Sophia Books
An imprint of Rudolf Steiner Press
Hillside House, The Square
Forest Row, East Sussex
RH18 5ES

www.rudolfsteinerpress.com

First published under the title *Breathing the Spirit* by Rudolf Steiner Press in 2002 and reprinted in 2007
This revised edition 2018

Rudolf Steiner's verses are selected from the following volumes of the *Rudolf Steiner Gesamtausgabe* ('GA'), his Collected Works published in the original German by Rudolf Steiner Verlag, Dornach: GA 40 *Wahrspruchworte*, GA 267 *Seelenübungen* and GA 268 *Mantrische Sprüche*. This authorized volume is published by permission of the Rudolf Steiner Nachlassverwaltung, Dornach

A catalogue record for this book is available from the British Library

ISBN 978 1 85584 554 1

Cover by Morgan Creative featuring an image © Valentin Valkov
Typeset by DP Photosetting, Aylesbury, Bucks.
Printed and bound in Great Britain by 4Edge Ltd., Essex

Contents

	Introduction	7
I	THE DAY'S BREATH	9
1	Morning	11
2	Noon and afternoon	31
3	Evening	39
4	Night	59
II	LIGHTING UP THE YEAR	71
1	Spring	75
2	Summer	83
3	Autumn	95
4	Winter	103
	Notes	117
	Index of first lines	119

A breath from the spirit world,
waking into the body,
falling asleep to leave the body,
is how the true being of the I
experiences itself alternately.

In spirit weaving's respiration I
am as air in the lung-body:
I am not lung; no, but the air that's breathed;
yet lung is what's aware of me.
If I grasp this I perceive
myself in the spirit of the world.

Introduction

The simplest things often contain the greatest depths: we do not need scientists or philosophers to tell us that we wake up in the morning and fall asleep at night. But this deceptively simple rhythm of life, in which we follow the natural cycle of our earth's rotation (yet are of course free to ignore it if we wish by 'burning midnight oil'—see verse on page 50!) also contains a mystery which scientists and philosophers are hard put to answer. What really happens when we sleep, dream and wake?

The meditations gathered in the first section of this book all relate to the breathing rhythm of waking and sleeping, through which our spirit enters and leaves its earthly habitation in a continual cycle. As we dwell on (and in) these verses, we can gain a sense that the journey we pass through each day is a microcosm of greater, longer rhythms: descending from a world of spirit into the vessel of the body as we do at birth, and ascending back to that world of spirit as happens at death; becoming conscious and active on earth and living into our senses; and losing consciousness (most of us) in non-physical realms where spiritual activity has its true home. These meditations can accompany us each day on the smaller echo of our greater journey, gently reminding us where we have come from, and where we might be going.

The second section—'Lighting up the Year'—addresses our passage through a greater cycle of sleeping and waking—that of nature's changing seasons. The meditations gathered in this section trace a path through human experience of the year, very much focusing on our *inner* response to outer changes in nature. We not only follow these changes but also experience a polarity with them. For instance, our inner life can be most intense and awake in winter, when least sustained by natural forces of growth—rather like being wide awake in the middle of the night. The meaning of some of these verses is not always immediately transparent; they repay long pondering, and then they can gradually become interwoven with our own experience of the year's course, helping the light of spirit to shine in our daylight, and vice versa.

Matthew Barton

I

THE DAY'S BREATH

1

Morning

At the moment of waking

Self in the spirit
you hold sway in the spheres
you shine in light
you work in fire
you are wisdom, beauty, strength,
you are I
I wish to be you.

My eye opens
and receives the light of day,
after night's peace has strengthened me;
my heart, be strong in will and powerfully feel
how courage and life from God's wide world
pour, give themselves into my limbs.
Let me know at every moment
that God's high powers sustain and bless
everything I can feel within me
and strength enables me to attain.

More radiant than the sun,
purer than snow,
finer than the ether
is the self
the spirit in my heart.
This self am I. I am this self.[1]

Light's radiant forms,
glorious ocean of the spirit:
the soul leaves you.
In the divine it rested,
rested its being;
into vessels of earthly existence
consciously steps my I.[2]

I will be
I will live
I will rest
I will find myself
in the soul of the world
in the spirit of the world
in the God-core of the world.[3]

In the pure rays of the light
shines the God-hood of the world.
In the pure fire of the ether
streams the I-hood's mighty power.
I rest in the spirit of the world,
I will always find myself
In the eternal spirit of the world.

Steadfast I place myself into the world.
With certain steps I walk through life.
Love I tend in the core of my being.
Hope I put in all I do.
Peace leads me to my goal,
peace leads me into the world.
Wisdom I seek in all my thinking.[4]

In my heart
lives the strength
enlivening me;
if I take hold of it
with my will
it will sustain me
sound and well through life.

I think of my heart
it enlivens me
it warms me;
I trust wholly in
the eternal self
that works in me,
sustaining me.

My heart
take up Christ's mercy.
Warm my soul,
spirit in my blood,
so that I become
strong and well
to work in the world.[5]

The sun's bright light
illumines day
after dark night:
the soul's strength now
awakens from
sleep's quiet rest:
you, my soul,
give thanks to the light,
within it shines
the power of God;
you, my soul, arise,
do spirited deeds.

In the far-flung universe
also stirred the strength
which gave my soul existence.
So this strength I'll sense, remember,
trusting, hope that it will bring me light
to shine continually in my life.

In wide universal spaces
creative cosmic spirit weaves;
from wide universal spaces
into my soul shines living strength.

My eye takes pleasure in
the shining sun's bright glow;
so, my soul, be glad also
at God's spirit that indwells all,
as the invisible sun that shines
lovingly to every being.[6]

I look into the world—
the shining sun,
the glittering stars,
the solid rocks;
the plants alive and growing,
the creatures sensing, living;
this world, where our souls
give spirit dwelling-place;
I look into my soul
that dwells alive within.

The spirit of God weaves through
light of sun and soul
out in the world's expanse,
within, in depths of soul.

To you O spirit of God
I turn and ask
that blessing and strength may grow
within me, flow into
all my learning and
all my work.[7]

Seeing the sun
I think God's spirit,
moving my hand
God's soul lives in me,
taking a step
God's will walks in me.
In all people whom I see
God's soul lives;
and lives also
in creature, plant and stone.
Fear can never touch me
when I think God's spirit,
when I feel God's soul,
when I walk in God's will.[8]

Radiant sun-star,
shining home
of world-forming beings,
open for me
heart and sensing soul
so that I may be strong in time and eternity.

2

Noon and afternoon

Grace at mealtimes

In the deep, dark earth, plants stir
green shoots sprout in the vital air
fruits ripen through the sun's bright power;

so stirs the soul in the shrine of the heart
so sprouts the spirit's strength in the light of the
world
so ripens our human strength in the brightness of
God.

Sunlight streams through
far breadths of space,
birdsong rings out
through open fields of air,
the gift and grace of plants sprout from
the being of earth;
and, in gratitude, human souls
lift themselves to the spirits of the world.[9]

In my heart streams
the strength of the sun,
in my soul works
the warmth of the world.

I will breathe
the strength of the sun

I will feel
the warmth of the world.

Sun strength fills me,
warmth of the world penetrates me.

The sun shines down
into matter's dark;
so shines the spirit's
all-healing essence
down into soul-dark
of my human being.
Whenever I reflect
on its strong power
with the right warmth of heart,
it glows through me
with its spirit midday power.

Afternoon rest

Now I lie down to rest
I am at rest
I hear myself;
in rest I hear myself
in great rest I hear myself
   I stay at rest.

* * *

My rest is at an end
I begin once more
   to move.

I breathe the power of life out of blue distances

I breathe back my own self into blue distances

3

Evening

In the airy light of spirit land
blossom the roses of the soul,
and their red streams out
into earth's heaviness—in us
is condensed into heart form,
raying back in the vigorous blood
to spirit pastures once again
as earth's pink and rosy red.

To the sign of the world spirit
let my soul lift longingly . . .

In the bright red, rosy light
I see the power of the spirit.

In the deep ground of my soul
let this selfsame spirit power
wake: sustain, hold, guide and lead me.

If I look around me
I see the sun's
deeds of light;
If I look into me
I see the soul's
spirit will.
I am light in the spirit,
spirit in light.

See the universally active
eternal powers
of the stars in their stillness.

Human beings need inner faith,
faith in the guidance of spiritual beings.
Upon this faith we can build up
our eternal being's existence
and thereby strengthen and stream through
sense-life with eternal light.

From my head to my feet
I am the image of God,
from my heart to my hands
I feel God's breath,
speaking with my mouth
I follow God's will.
When I see God
everywhere, in mother, father,
in all loving people,
in creatures, stones,
no fear is mine,
just love for all
that is around me.[10]

Prayer at the ringing of evening bells

To wonder at beauty,
guard the truth,
honour what's noble,
resolve to do good:
this leads human beings
in life to their goal,
in deeds to what's right,
in feelings to peace,
in thinking to light;
and teaches them trust
in the working of God
in all that exists
in the universe,
in the innermost soul.[11]

I look into the starry world—
and understand the stars' bright gleam
when I can see within it God's
wisdom guiding worlds.
I look into my heart within—
and understand my beating heart
when I can sense within it God's
love guiding human beings.
I know nothing of the starry world
and nothing of my beating heart
unless I see, sense God; for he
led my soul into this world ...[12]

All the stars in the sky
speak of spirit's beauty;
the sun in cosmic space
speaks of spirit's power;
the moon in night's dark cloak
speaks of spirit's paths.[13]

Lamp

In my physical body
    as vessel
is my etheric body
    as oil;
from this is nourished, as is the flame,
    my soul body;
and shining like the flame's light lives my I.

Out of the light of space
sense brightness fades;
into the light of the soul
may spirit brightness dawn.
Seek it my soul,
find it my soul
in truth, clarity, love.

Wisdom I seek in all my thinking.
peace leads me into the world,
peace leads me to my goal.
Hope I put in all I do.
Love I tend in the core of my being.
With certain steps I walk through life,
steadfast I place myself into the world.[14]

In the distance beckons spirit image
and the spirit image is with God
and a God is the spirit image;
in him is the living I
and the living I is the light of human beings.

My soul
sense Christ's grace;
from my heart
Christ bears me
into the land of spirit
and gives me
strength for true life.[15]

I am the self
the self am I,
the spirit in my heart
is the self.
It is finer than the ether,
purer than snow,
more radiant than the sun.[16]

In the God-core of the world,
in the spirit of the world,
in the soul of the world
I will find myself;
will rest in it,
live in it,
have my being in it.[17]

My I consciously steps
out of vessels of earthly existence
to rest in the essence of worlds.
It strives towards the divine.
Soul, attain this realm,
the spirit's glorious ocean,
light's radiant forms.[18]

4

Night

To live in the spirit
and breathe the spirit
is the soul's urge.
This will come to me when I
sleep, my eyes
closing protectively.

My soul departs now
from the sense world
into the spirit world.
Strengthened by forces
that flow to it from the spirit world,
it will return in the morning
into the sense world.

When my eyes close
and depart from the light of day
after daily work's been done,
let me feel powerfully
how God's wide world
mercifully takes me into itself;
how high powers of God eternally
guard and sustain my courage and life.

Primal powers hold me,
spirits of fire free me,
spirits of light illumine me
so that I reach towards spirit life
so that I feel beings of soul
so that I traverse uncertainties
so that I stand above the abyss.

In me let Christ live
and change my breath
and warm the course of my blood
and shine into my soul being.

The stars shine
it is night
stillness fills space
all is quiet
I feel the stillness
I feel the quiet
in my heart
in my head
God speaks
Christ speaks.[19]

Prayer

O powers in the world of spirit,
when I step out of my physical body
let me be conscious in the world of light,
be in the light,
so I can observe my own light-body;
and let the might of ahrimanic powers
not hold sway too strongly over me,
so that they hinder me from seeing
what unfolds in my body of light.

At our present times on earth
we once more need spiritual content
in the words we speak;
for in sleep, residing beyond our body,
soul and spirit retain of speech what bears
signs of the spirit.
For sleeping people must
come into dialogue with the angeloi.
But these only take up words'
spirit, not material content.
If we lack this dialogue,
our whole being suffers injury.[20]

I am in cosmic expanse
and my own being expands:
my eye is the dome of heaven
and my nerve-endings, life threads, are
stars—the stars in my world eye;
and my pupil is the moon.
I see the firmament,
and the firmament is a point,
the firmament is my soul,
my I-bearing soul.

In the God-hood of the world
    rests my being;
in the spirit of the world
    rests my soul;
in the soul of the world
    rests my spirit;
now and for ever.

II

LIGHTING UP THE YEAR

Through the year the seasons pass
from summer's strong growth
to resting winter earth.
And in our own life too,
from waking strength we pass
to sleep's deep peace; and yet
through both sleep and waking lives
the spirit-filled soul. And so too does
the soul of earth live spiritually in
all changes from summer to winter time.

1

Spring

Expectation of spring

Into our inner being pours
the riches of the senses;
the world spirit finds itself
within the mirror of the human eye
which from world spirit must draw strength
to recreate itself anew.[21]

Sun's shining ray,
light-sparkling,
wings its way here.

The blossom bride,
blushing into colour
greets it gladly.

Trustingly
sun-ray confides
in earth's daughter, telling

how sun forces,
sprung from spirit,
eavesdrop on sphere-music where
gods reside.

the blossom bride,
glittering with colour,
hearkens, pondering, to
light's fire music.

Easter

Into human souls I'll guide
sense of spirit, to willingly
waken in hearts the Easter word;

with human spirits I will think
warmth of soul, that powerfully
they may feel the risen one;

brightly in death's apparent face
shines spirit understanding's earthly flame;
and self becomes the eye and ear of worlds.

Stand at the gateway to human life:
see cosmic words clear written there.

Live in the interior of the human soul:
feel world beginning in its sphere.

Think of the human being's earthly end:
find in it the spirit's turning tide.

Easter mood

When from wide universal spaces sun
speaks to human senses and
joy that rises from soul depths
unites with light in seeing, then
out of selfhood's husk our thoughts
draw into far distances and dimly
join our being to spirit's being.[22]

2

Summer

Summer will

You my head's
forming soul forces,
you fill my own existence,
you penetrate from my being
out into world breadths
and unite me with
world-creating powers.

Whitsun

Being weaves with being in breadths of space,
being follows being through cycles of time;
if you wish to leave the transient realm
and enter the sphere of eternity,
forge a strong bond with knowledge, for
only then you'll find what is eternal
in you and outside you—
beyond all breadths of space,
beyond time's ever-circling course.

Only where sense knowledge ends
stands the gateway, opening
the soul to living reality;
the soul creates the key
when it grows strong within itself
in the struggle which worldly forces
wage on their own ground with
human beings' powers;
when by its own means soul drives off
the sleep that, at the senses' furthest limit,
shrouds powers of knowledge in spiritual night.

Midsummer. Uriel imagination

Mysteries of the heights

See our weaving:
the shining, stirring
warming pulse of living.

Mysteries of the depths

Let what sustains earth,
and form created in breath
live as true essence holding sway.

Mysteries of the centre and of the human interior

Feel your human bones
shone through with heavenly tones
in joined worlds' reign.

Like a cosmic affirmation of these mysteries, sounding into the whole as though with organ and trumpet tones

Substance grows dense, is crystallized,
addressed and mended are errors and lies,
hearts are sifted, clarified.

The sun's light strengthens earth's creation,
Truth's sunlight strengthens the human heart.

St John's mood

The glorious, radiant light of worlds
urges me from depths of soul
to deliver my own life's godly forces up,
setting them free in universal flight;
to leave myself, and trusting seek myself
only in world light and world warmth.[23]

Out of the heights there streams
the sun’s bright light;
yet spirit forces live
in limpid, clear sunshine.
And there dwells in us
our own heart warmth within;
yet soul forces stream
out of the heart’s warm core.
In sunlight’s spirit reigns
God’s wisdom everywhere;
in warm strength of heart
soul love prevails, holds sway.

Sun, ray-bearer,
your light's material power
conjures life from the earth's
immeasurable, rich depths.

Heart, soul-bearer,
your light's spirit power
conjures life from the human being's
immeasurable inner depths.

If I look into the sun,
its light speaks radiantly to me
from the spirit that full of grace
prevails, penetrates world essence.

If I feel into my heart,
spirit speaks its own intrinsic word
from the human being it loves
through all time and eternity.

Looking upwards I can see
in the sun's bright disc above,
the mighty, pulsing world heart;

looking inwards I can feel
in the warm beat of my heart,
the ensouled sun of the human being.

My soul, follow the light of the sun;
my soul is a being of light,
following the sun it finds,
as light, the light.

See, my eye,
the sun's pure rays
in the earth's form being;

See, my heart,
the sun's spirit powers
in the water's pulsing waves;

See, my soul,
the sun's world will
in air-currents flickering shimmer;

See, my spirit,
the sun's god-being
in fire's streams of love.

3

Autumn

The earth body and warmth soul

The earth body,
longing for spirit,
lives in withering.

The seed spirits,
substance-compressed,
take up strength.

And warmth fruits from
the far-spread breadths of space
fortify earth life.

And earthly senses,
the deep-gazers,
see future things
within creating form.

The spirits of space,
eternally breathing,
look peacefully upon
earthly weaving.

Michaelmas

Battling spirit forces
strive in substance.
They do not find substance,
but only themselves.
They glide above the natural,
living within themselves,
breathing Michael strength.

Michael imagination

Spiritual powers springing from
sun-forces: shining, world-grace bestowing;
divine, creative thinking destines you
to be Michael's dress of rays.

He, the messenger of Christ, endows you with
holy world will, sustaining us;
you, the bright beings of ether worlds,
bear to human beings the word of Christ.

So appears the Christ-proclaimer
to patient, longing, thirsting souls:
for them your shining word streams onwards
into the future age of spirit man.

You, pupils of spirit knowledge,
take up Michael's wise direction,
take up the loving word of world will
actively into your striving souls.

Michael's sword. Meteoric iron

O man,
you form it to serve you,
you reveal its material worth
in many of your creations.
Yet it will only make you sound and whole
when is revealed to you
its spirit's high power.

Michaelmas mood

Nature, your mothering being
I bear within my will;
and my will's power of fire
steels the promptings of my spirit,
giving birth to selfhood's sense
so that I bear me in myself.[24]

4

Winter

Winter will

O world pictures
you wing your way
from breadths of space.
You strive towards me,
penetrate my head's
thinking forces.

Winter solstice

Earth blocks the sun,
forces of vision compel
from earth's elements
liberated sight.

See the sun
at deep midnight
use stones to build
in the lifeless ground.

So find in decline
and in death's night
creation's new beginning
morning's fresh force.

Let the heights reveal
divine word of gods;
the depths sustain and nurture
the stronghold of peace.

Living in darkness
engender a sun;
weaving in substance
see spirit's bliss.

Christmas mood

As though released from a spell I feel
the spirit child in the lap of the soul.
May it, in the heart's bright light,
engender the holy word of worlds,
hope's heavenly fruit,
that grows, rejoicing, into world distances
out of my being's ground of God.[25]

In the deep ground of our soul
lives, sure to triumph, spirit sun;
true forces of our feeling mind
can sense it in the inward life
of winter; and heart's springing hope
sees the triumph of sun spirit
shine in blessed Christmas light,
as an image of the highest life
in deep winter's darkest night.

Divine revelation in spirit heights:
peace, continually more peace
to all souls living on the earth
who are of good will.

The eye of soul reflects
the hopeful light of worlds,
hearkening to the spirit, wisdom
speaks in human hearts:
the Father's everlasting love
sends the Son to earth,
who full of grace sheds light
of heaven on human paths.

Sunrise of humanity's evolution
on earth: great mystery
on Golgotha's heights.
In the Christmas light
dawn's radiance shines;
revere the soul in this
daybreak's gentle light:
our own being's spirit-kinned
power and source of life.

Stars once spoke to us,
their silence now is world destiny;
awareness of this silence
can cause us earthly human beings pain.

But in mute stillness ripens
what we speak to the stars;
awareness of this speech
can strengthen our spiritual core.[26]

At the crux of time,
the spirit light of worlds entered
earthly being's onward flow;
darkness of night
had held dominion;
bright light of day
streamed into human souls;
light bringing warmth
to simple shepherd hearts;
light that illumines
kings' wise heads—
God-filled light,
Christ sun,
O warm
our hearts;
illumine
our heads;

so that good may grow
from everything that we
start from our hearts,
from everything that we
try through our heads
to guide purposefully.[27]

The earth's soul sleeps
in summer's heat;
then the sun's mirror blazes
in the outer world.

The earth's soul wakes
in winter's cold;
then the true sun shines
spiritually within.

In summer's joyful day
earth sleeps deep;
in winter's holy night
earth rouses, wakes.

Notes

1 A companion verse to the evening verse on page 55.
2 A companion verse to the evening verse on page 57.
3 A companion verse to the evening verse on page 56.
4 A companion verse to the evening verse on page 52.
5 A companion to the evening verse on page 54.
6 Given to an eleven-year-old boy.
7 Morning school-verse for older children.
8 For young children.
9 This could also be used as a grace at mealtimes.
10 For young children.
11 For a seven-year-old boy.
12 For a nine-year-old boy.
13 For a seven-year-old girl.
14 A companion verse to the morning verse on page 18.
15 A companion verse to the morning verse on page 22.
16 A companion verse to the morning verse on page 15.
17 A companion verse to the morning verse on page 17.
18 A companion verse to the morning verse on page 16.
19 For a ten-year-old boy.
20 From a letter to Marie Steiner.
21 From the *Calendar of the Soul.*

[22] From the *Calendar of the Soul*.

[23] From the *Calendar of the Soul*.

[24] From the *Calendar of the Soul*.

[25] From the *Calendar of the Soul*.

[26] Given to Marie Steiner on 25 December 1922.

[27] This meditation, given on 25 December 1923, was part of the core 'Foundation Stone' meditation given at the so-called Christmas Foundation Meeting, at which the Anthroposophical Society was re-founded in a wholly new form.

Index of first lines

A breath from the spirit world, 6
All the stars in the sky, 49
As though released from a spell I feel, 108
At our present times on earth, 67
At the crux of time, 114
Battling spirit forces, 98
Being weaves with being in breadths of space, 86
Divine revelation in spirit heights, 110
Earth blocks the sun, 106
From my head to my feet, 46
Human beings need inner faith, 45
I am in cosmic expanse, 68
I am the self, 55
I breathe the power of life out of blue distances, 38
If I look around me, 43
I look into the starry world, 48
I look into the world, 27
In my heart, 20
In my heart streams, 35
In my physical body, 50
In the airy light of spirit land, 41
In the deep, dark earth, plants stir, 33
In the deep ground of our soul, 109
In the distance beckons spirit image, 53
In the far-flung universe, 24
In the God-core of the world, 56

In the God-hood of the world, 69
In the pure rays of the light, 18
Into human souls I'll guide, 79
Into our inner being pours, 77
In wide universal spaces, 25
I think of my heart, 21
I will be, 17
Light's radiant forms, 16
More radiant than the sun, 15
My eye opens, 14
My eye takes pleasure in, 26
My heart take up Christ's mercy, 22
My I consciously steps, 57
My soul departs now, 62
My soul, follow the light of the sun, 93
My soul sense Christ's grace, 54
Mysteries of the heights, 88
Nature, your mothering being, 101
Now I lie down to rest, 37
O man, you form it to serve you, 100
Only where sense knowledge ends, 87
O powers in the world of spirit, 66
Out of the heights there streams, 91
Out of the light of space, 51
O world pictures, 105
Primal powers hold me, 64
Radiant sun-star, 29
Seeing the sun, 28
See, my eye, 94

See the sun at deep midnight, 107
See the universally active, 44
Self in the spirit, 13
Spiritual powers springing from, 99
Stand at the gateway to human life, 80
Stars once spoke to us, 113
Steadfast I place myself into the world, 19
Sunlight streams through, 34
Sun, ray-bearer, 92
Sunrise of humanity's evolution, 112
Sun's shining ray, 78
The earth body, 97
The earth's soul sleeps, 115
The eye of soul reflects, 111
The glorious, radiant light of worlds, 90
The stars shine, 65
The sun's bright light, 23
The sun shines down, 36
The sun's light strengthens earth's creation, 89
Through the year the seasons pass, 73
To live in the spirit, 61
To the sign of the world spirit, 42
To wonder at beauty, 47
When from wide universal spaces sun, 81
When my eyes close, 63
Wisdom I seek in all my thinking, 52
You my head's, 85